Potted History

It was obvious that the DC-4 was in trouble. It had just taken off from Geneva-Cointrin and the landing gear, instead of retracting, stayed stubbornly down – this looked serious, and I wondered what was coming next. The DC-4 climbed slowly away from the runway and then, belatedly, the undercarriage folded away, but the machine went into the circuit with the obvious intention of landing back. Down came the wheels again, but fire tenders and rescue vehicles were racing out to the runway as the DC-4 turned into the long approach against a majestic background of Jura mountains.

Seen against the natural beauty of its surroundings, the large machine looked small, insignificant, and, for all I knew, about to become a death trap for all on board. The emergency vehicles alongside the runway showed that all was not well, and I guessed that there was concern about the undercarriage collapsing. I felt sick with apprehension as the DC-4 approached the runway, then apprehension quickly turned to relief as the undercarriage held at touchdown and the bird came to a halt safely. I was surprised that the airliner, with its faulty landing gear, was taxied back with its passengers on board – they could have been disembarked on the runway and collected by coach. As the DC-4 taxied in, I noticed liquid dripping from a wing, so perhaps fuel had been jettisoned to get the aircraft down to a safe landing weight.

Let's go back to the 'thirties when the DC-4 story began. Several companies produced airliners in those days and, by 1938, the British had Armstrong Whitworth, de Havilland and Short. In France there was Bloch and Dewoitine The Germans had Focke Wulf and Junkers, while Italy's major airliner builder was Savoia-Marchetti. But the USA was the world's airliner centre *par excellence*, with the highest production rates, thanks mainly to Douglas, Lockheed and Boeing.

However, the one company which stood head and shoulders above any other on the world stage was Douglas, a firm propelled to the top of the league by the sheer technical excellence and commercial 'rightness' of its DC-2 and DC-3 machines. These were twin-engined machines, and, as early as 1935 when the DC-3 first flew, airlines were already looking ahead to operating four-engined airliners. Douglas and Boeing proposed designs, while Lockheed joined in somewhat later. Douglas' contender, the DC-4, was initially backed by five major US airlines, although by the time it first flew, on 7 June 1938, the DC-4's sheer complexity lost it support and, after certification and route proving flights, development was discontinued due to its poor economics and performance.

But this setback, far from eliminating Douglas from the four-engined market, was the start of a golden era for Douglas transports. Because, with support from American, Eastern and United Air Lines, Douglas developed a smaller and less complex aircraft with better economics to replace the unfortunate DC-4E (as it became

known). The new machine was, confusingly, also called the DC-4 despite being a completely different aircraft.

The redesigned DC-4 was about 25 per cent lighter than its ponderous DC-4E predecessor, and was planned to carry 42 day passengers. Power came from four Pratt & Whitney R-2000 14-cylinder radials, each giving 1,450 hp. The type first flew in February 1942, and, as the USA was, by then, engaged in WW2 the DC-4 went straight into service as a heavy long-range military transport, a role for which the DC-4, known as the C-54 in military guise, was admirably suited.

Douglas had produced a winner, and about 1,200 C-54s were built, and, post-war, the type was a mainstay of the Berlin Airlift. With the return of peace in 1945, numerous ex-military C-54s were converted into civil DC-4s for the airlines – which, unfortunately for Douglas, depressed the market for new DC-4s and only 79 new machines were built as DC-4-1009s. Airlines clamoured for DC-4s, either new or converted from C-54s, as they set up operations after WW2. US airlines buying DC-4s included Pan Am, Delta, American, American Overseas Airlines, Eastern, Western, Northwest and United, among others. Outside the USA, DC-4s went to SILA, Sabena, KLM, Air France, ABA, DNL, Iberia, Swissair, ANA, TAA, SAA etc.

On 23 October 1945, American Overseas Airlines inaugurated commercial transatlantic landplane services flying a DC-4 from New York to Hurn Airport (Bournemouth) via Newfoundland and Shannon. Other airlines followed suit and by 1949 Air France, SAS, KLM, Sabena, Pan Am and Swissair etc were flying routine transatlantic services with their DC-4s. The DC-4 also opened up long-haul routes in other parts of the world, and became a mainstay of American domestic long-haul services. In 1948, at the age of seven, I flew from Geneva to London (Northolt, I think) in a Swissair DC-4. To fly in a large four-engined aircraft in those days carried a certain *cachet*.

An interesting variant of the DC-4 was the Canadair-built version powered by Rolls-Royce Merlins. These engines gave the stately DC-4 a useful performance increase, raising cruise from 227 mph to 289 mph. The prototype flew in July 1946, and, unlike the DC-4, civil versions of the Canadair machine were pressurised and were flown by TCA (20), BOAC (22) and CPA(4). The RCAF bought 23 unpressurised C-54GM versions. Another interesting, if hideous, version of the DC-4 was the Carvair, a conversion designed as a car ferry and first flying in June 1961; 20 of these strange-looking machines were produced, all being converted from used DC-4s – the only affordable way of producing such a specialised machine.

Excellent aircraft though it was, the DC-4 was no match for the Lockheed Constellation, and it had a relatively short innings as a first line long-hauler. Fortunately, the DC-4 was capable of being enlarged and developed into the pressurised DC-6, with 2,100 hp Pratt & Whitney R-2800 radials instead of the DC-4's 1,450 hp engines. Although introduced into airline service over a year after the Connie, the DC-6 was an effective competitor. The DC-6 prototype flew on 15 February 1946, and, with its span of 117 ft 6 ins and length of 100 ft 7 in, it was about the same size as the competing Constellation. The first DC-6s were delivered on 24 November 1946, simultaneously, to American Airlines and United Airlines, and services began after five months of route proving and training flights, thus starting a brilliant career for the aircraft. Accommodation varied between 48 and 86 passengers and the aircraft was one of the first airliners, along with the Connie, with a cruise in excess of the all-important 300 mph threshold.

An early problem with the DC-6 resulted in two in-flight fires in 1947. The aircraft had petrol-fired combustion heaters for cabin heating and de-icing. Initial problems due to venting of fuel into the cabin heater air intake caused the fatal crash of United Airlines N37510, with the tragic loss of passengers and crew. But, an American Air Lines DC-6 was luckier, landing on fire, but safely at Gallup, New Mexico on 11 November 1947. All DC-6s were grounded for four months while the fault was cured.

A total of 175 DC-6s were built and all except one were sold to airlines in no less than ten countries, the single exception being for presidential use in the USA as a C-118 named *Independence*. Airlines in the USA bought 126 DC-6s and the largest orders came from United and American which took 50 and 46 aircraft, respectively. Braniff received nine machines, one of which was the final DC-6 to be built and was delivered on 2 November 1951; seven went to Delta, and National and Panagra received eight and six respectively.

Sabena bought five DC-6s, eight were delivered to KLM, and 17 went to SAS. Linee Aeree Italiane (LAI), which merged with Alitalia in 1957, took four. Outside Europe and the USA, six DC-6s went to Flota Aerea Mercante Argentina (FAMA). Mexicana took three and Philippine Air Lines (PAL) bought five.

Douglas stretched the DC-6 into the DC-6A cargo aircraft, which flew on 29 September 1949 with P&W R-2800-CB16 engines uprated by 14 per cent to 2,400 hp. A total of 75 DC-6As were built, and the type went to Slick Airways, American Air Lines, Flying Tiger, Northeast, Pan Am, Canadian Pacific, KLM, and Sabena, among other operators. The USAF bought 101 military versions of the DC-6A (C-118A) as personnel and logistics transports for the Military Air Transport Service (MATS). These aircraft could, alternatively, carry 74 passengers, 60 stretcher cases or 27,000 lb of cargo. The US Navy, also, bought 65 versions of the DC-6A known as R6D-1s

The final DC-6 development was the highly-regarded DC-6B passenger airliner which, with the same dimensions as the DC-6A, was offered with either R-2800-CB16 engines of 2,400 hp each, or with 2,500 hp R-2800-CB17s. The first DC-6B went into service with American Airlines on 29 April 1951, and, of the 287 DC-6Bs built, 283 were delivered to 29 airlines in an incredible 20 countries. Some of the DC-6B's operators are given in the main text later on; suffice it to say that Douglas had produced exactly what the airlines wanted, an aircraft with an excellent combination of performance, reliability, operating economics and ease of maintenance.

A total of 704 examples of the DC-6 series were built, and the final version, the DC-6B, stayed in production until 1958. The DC-6B was probably the best all-round piston airliner ever built – and, along with the Connie with jet-stack exhausts, was one of the noisiest!

In the meantime, responding to an American Airlines requirement, Douglas developed the DC-6B into the DC-7, powered by the 3,250 hp Wright Turbo Compound radial, notable for its power recovery turbines driven by exhaust gases. The DC-7 was Douglas' answer to the Lockheed Super Constellation, and American Airlines initially ordered 25 DC-7s worth a total of $40 million. Douglas was unconvinced that the DC-7 would sell, but the American Airlines order launched the DC-7, and the airline paid for most of the development costs.

The DC-7, looking very similar to its DC-6B parent, first flew on 18 May 1953, and American Airlines introduced the type on the New York - Los Angeles service on 29 November 1953. In the event, American took 34 machines, and other buyers included Delta, National and United.

Competition between Douglas and Lockheed forced the pace of development of both Super Connie and DC-7, leading to the DC-7B which flew in October 1954, enabling Pan Am to start its non-stop New York to London services on 13 June 1955. Like the Lockheed 1049C Super Connie, Pan Am's DC-7Bs could only fly the Atlantic non-stop in the eastbound direction due to prevailing winds. The DC-7B was delivered to Panagra, Eastern, Pan Am, American, Continental, National and SAA.

Competitive pressure was on for non-stop transatlantic services in both directions, and Douglas introduced the DC-7C Seven Seas. This was the first airliner able to fly the transatlantic run non-stop in either direction against prevailing winds, giving it the edge over the competing Lockheed 1049G Super Connie. Pan Am put the DC-7C to work on 1 June 1956; power had risen to a massive 3,400 hp per engine from the uprated Wright Turbo Compound 18EA1s. In addition to Pan Am, DC-7Cs were operated by BOAC, KLM, SAS, Swissair, Braniff, Panair do Brasil, Mexicana, Sabena, Northeast, Northwest, Alitalia, TAI and JAL.

The DC-7C, along with the Lockheed 1649 Starliner, marked the swansong of the piston airliner era, brought to a premature end by the arrival of the jetliner, and both the DC-7C and Starliner had but a short innings before being overtaken by the Boeing 707 and Comet 4 jetliners in 1958. And so came to an end one of the most colourful periods of commercial aviation, a time when the piston-engined airliner had reached a high degree of development, able to fly non-stop safely and reliably between European capitals and the New World as a matter of routine. Jetliners were quiet inside and stunningly fast, but they never had the same aura as piston airliners except in the early days of jet travel.

****

In 1935 Douglas and United Airlines held initial discussions for a four-engined airliner with twice the DC-3's capacity and a 2,200 mile range. Five US airlines, American, Eastern, Pan Am, TWA and United each put forward $100,000 towards the design and construction of a prototype DC-4E, as the aircraft became known. A remarkably large aircraft for its day with its 138 ft 3 in span and length of 97 ft 7 in, the DC-4E was designed to meet a spec defined by United, specifying a capacity of 40 passengers, a 54,000 lb take-off weight and a 175 mph cruise. The only example built is shown on the right in with some Douglas B-18 bombers, the DC-4E looking rather like a Constellation, with its

The one and only Douglas DC-4E being built; it was not a success   *M J Hooks*

four engines, triple fins, tricycle undercarriage and curvaceous fuselage. The three fins, incidentally, were used instead of a larger single fin so that the aircraft would fit into existing hangars. In the event, the machine was built as a 52-seater weighing in at 65,000 lb, and Douglas and the five participating airlines signed a production order for 40 aircraft.

Not only was the new aircraft a major step forward in design due to its sheer size and carrying capacity, because its Pratt & Whitney R-2180 Twin Hornet engines were new also, and, at 1,450 hp each, were extremely powerful at a time, when 1,000 hp was a high output for a production engine. The Twin Hornets were 14 cylinder two-row radials, and were developed especially for the large new DC-4E. The value of high-altitude flight for commercial aircraft, where low density air gives less drag and therefore greater economy, and allows above-weather flight, could be exploited with the pressurisation system planned for the production DC-4E. We take pressurisation for granted on modern airliners, but it was

This may be a mock-up of the DC-4E's spacious interior   *M J Hooks*

in its infancy during the 'thirties and a very new concept.

With its swept wing and other characteristics, the DC-4E, not surprisingly, looked like an enlarged four-engined DC-3 with a tricycle undercarriage and triple fins. As a portent of things to come, the machine was fitted with APUs, as are modern airliners, for providing ground power. This was not a normal feature on airliners of an earlier generation, which used portable 'plug-in' ground power units.

As can be seen from the 1939 photograph on the left, probably a mock-up, the passenger cabin was roomy, quite unlike the cramped conditions in modern airliners, underlining the fact that airline flying during the 'thirties was for the chosen and demanding few. What the photo does not show, in addition to the main passenger cabin, are the two lounges and stateroom! Yet, although large aircraft made such

The DC-4E's cancellation led to the excellent DC-4   *B Robertson*

luxury possible, it was the introduction of large aircraft, started off by the DC-4E, which gave the economies of scale making possible the mass air transport that we have today, in which standards of service have necessarily become more basic than when the DC-4E was conceived.

Even before it was built, the DC-4E's sheer complexity lost it the financial support of Pan American and TWA, who veered towards the competing Boeing 307 Stratoliner, another four-engined, pressurised machine, but smaller than the DC-4E. The Boeing 307, incidentally, was developed from the B-17 bomber, i.e. B-17 wings, engines and tail unit mated to a passenger carrying fuselage. But back to the DC-4E. Despite the reduced development monies available resulting from Pan Am's and TWA's defection from the DC-4E programme, Douglas continued work and the DC-4E first flew on 7 June 1938 as NX18100.

After six months of development flying, the certificated aircraft, christened *Super Mainliner*, made extensive route proving flights with United Air Lines. However, the aircraft's complex systems, unsatisfactory operating economics and performance mitigated against it, and so development was discontinued with the agreement of the sponsoring airlines. In 1939, Douglas went ahead with a smaller four-engined airliner in the knowledge that American, Eastern and United Air Lines also believed that an airliner was needed with the same capacity as the DC-4E, but lighter and simpler, with less complex systems, easier maintenance and better operating economics.

This machine was a completely new aircraft, rather than a redesign of the DC-4E, yet, confusingly, it was called the DC-4 suggesting that the airliner was seen as a generic concept rather than as a specific aircraft. The two photographs on this page show the result. The redesigned DC-4 looked much more modern than its predecessor, with its straight tapered wing, single fin with dorsal extension, parallel-sided fuselage, and twin mainwheels, and it set a design trend which

American Overseas Airlines started post-WW2 transatlantic services with DC-4s   *M J Hooks*

A fine view of the DC-4's military C-54 forebear *MAP*

continued in airliners right up to the end of the piston era, evident in the DC-4's successors the DC-6 and DC-7 as well as in aircraft from other manufacturers such as the Vickers Viscount, Handley Page Hermes, Convair twins, Martin twins, Bristol Britannia and others. With its mainwheels retracting forward into the inner engine nacelles, the DC-4 established a design feature for piston airliners lasting until the jet age. The only indication of the DC-4's 'thirties origins was the single nosewheel, rather than the twin nosewheels used in other later large four-engined machines. The new DC-4 Skymaster had an oval-section fuselage and was about 25 per cent lighter than its rather ponderous, if graceful DC-4E predecessor. Wing area fell from the DC-4E's 2,155 ft^2 to 1,460 ft^2.

The DC-4 was planned to carry 40 day-passengers, or 28 by night, in two rows, one either side of a central aisle, each row being two seats wide. The idea of a different layout for day and night passengers seems quaint by modern standards, but that was what the demanding travelling public expected in those days. Predictably, Douglas offered the DC-4 with nine-cylinder Wright Cyclone R-1820 or 14-cylinder Pratt & Whitney R-1830 radials, of 1,000 hp and 1,050 hp respectively. These were the 'standard' engines used in large airliners at the time, although, in response to airline demand, the DC-4 standardised on 1,450 hp Pratt & Whitney R-2000 14-cylinder radials designed especially for it.

The DC-4 was a promising design, but the start of WW2 put a heavy demand for military aircraft on Douglas, from the US military as well as from France and Great Britain, both of whom had to make up the shortfall born of political neglect during the 'thirties, and now needed military aircraft urgently. The US War Department told Douglas to concentrate on military transport versions of its highly-successful DC-3 airliners, and to drop the DC-4, for which Douglas then had 61 orders. However Douglas managed to convince the War Department that the DC-4 would not interfere with war production, and continued with the DC-4 at reduced tempo.

In the event, DC-4s were taken over by the US military as C-54 military transports, and so the DC-4 entered service, not as an airliner, but as one of the best heavy military transport aircraft of WW2. The decision to proceed with the DC-4 as a military C-54 had been taken by the time the type made its first flight in February 1942, shortly after the USA had entered WW2 following the recent Japanese attack on Pearl Harbor. There was no prototype. The first machine was a production aircraft, and the soundness of the design ensured a trouble free machine with little, if any, of the development work

KLM was one of numerous airlines operating DC-4s after WW2 *M J Hooks*

normally needed before production can start. So, the USA entered the war with just the type of heavy long-range transport it needed to support its military operations. The DC-4, as the C-54, could hardly have been better conceived to meet this vital need, and proved its worth during WW2 as a military transport for personnel, troops, VIPs and cargo etc.

Carrying military personnel and cargo throughout the world, with routine transatlantic flights, the C-54 proved to be a sound and reliable machine with an excellent safety record. About 1,200 C-54s were

I saw an Air France DC-4 flying very low over the Sussex countryside in 1954   *M J Hooks*

built, and type continued in service for years after the war, as a military transport with the USAF. Perhaps the C-54's best-known work was post-war as a mainstay of the Berlin Airlift. I had good reason to remember the C-54, because in 1957 I was doing a week's summer camp at RAF Cranwell in the school cadet force. Going out for a walk with a fellow cadet on the airfield one fine Summer evening, we saw a couple of USAF C-54s parked nearby, and went over to investigate. Security was very lax in those days. There was no-one around, the door was open and there was even a portable stairway in place! Temptation got the better of us. It was worth the risk of a severe dressing down, and we sneaked aboard and had a good look round this Douglas masterpiece which, by then, was no longer a front-ranking long-hauler. I remember the upholstery in the cockpit roof, and the complex array of dials and controls. Also, the ground seemed far below from the top of the stairway. The following day, while attending a rather dull lecture, I heard the familiar and much-loved noise of the two C-54s taking off.

With the end of the war, there was considerable demand for the C-54 both from air forces, and, in civil DC-4-1009 guise, from the airlines. Douglas could offer early delivery to airlines and air forces from partially built C-54s, no longer required by the US military with the return of peace. However, airline demand could be met from cheaper military surplus C-54s converted into civil DC-4s. Douglas was a victim of its own success with the C-54, because it only managed to sell 79 newly built post-war DC-4-1009s thanks to surplus C-54s. Douglas and other organisations carried out conversions of ex-military C-54s into DC-4s for the airlines and, indeed, most of the DC-4s with which air travellers became so familiar post-war started life as C-54s. Pan Am bought no less than 92 converted aircraft, all bearing the *Clipper* name, as usual with Pan Am, particularly pleasant names being *Clippers Radiant* (N88922), *Gem of the Skies* (N58018), and *Guiding Star* (N88938), to mention but three.

An immaculate USAF C-54 military transport   *MAP*

Chicago and Southern Airlines, later to merge with Delta, operated six ex C-54s and an ex-Navy R5D-1. Delta bought seven ex C-54s between February and May 1946, and Delta's chief engineer J. F. Nycum designed a galley for these aircraft which Douglas adopted as standard equipment. Large four-engined airliners were a novelty in 1946 and when, one

Sabena's DC-4 OO-CBO surrounded by ground paraphernalia   *M J Hooks*

day, Delta made an airport announcement that *"Delta takes great pleasure in announcing the first of the fleet of DC-4 luxury Deltaliners"*, the airport lobby is said to have emptied as people rushed out to see this splendid new aircraft! Delta's DC-4s inaugurated services on 6 March 1946 on the 1,028 mile Chicago-Miami route, but Miami airport was worried about having to handle two of these large aircraft landing within the same hour! How times have changed.

Ex-military C-54s also went to American Overseas Airlines, and Swissair bought an ex-Pan Am C-54/DC-4 (ex-N88887) as HB-ILU. Western bought eight ex-military C-54s in 1946 and another one in 1954. There were other ex C-54 operators,, while airlines buying new DC-4s in the USA included Northwest, National, Waterman and Western, which took five in 1946 as NC10201 to '205. In Europe, new DC-4s went to SILA (forerunner of SAS), Sabena, KLM, Air France, ABA, DDL, Iberia, and Swissair. Other new DC-4 buyers included ANA and TAA in Australia, Aramco, and SAA, which received the last one to be produced.

By 1945, Atlantic flying was no longer newsworthy the way it had been in 1939 – just routine, thanks, in part, to the C-54, which had made 80,000 Atlantic crossings during the war with only three ditchings, one of which was deliberate.

An unmarked DC-4, possibly a military C-54 version   *M J Hooks*

It was logical that this transatlantic capability should be turned to commercial advantage when peace returned. So shortly after WW2, on 23 October 1945 American Overseas Airlines began commercial transatlantic landplane services, flying a DC-4 from New York to Hurn (Bournemouth) via Gander and Shannon. Other airlines followed suit and, by 1949, Air France, SAS, KLM, Sabena, Pan Am, and Swissair were regularly and safely making transatlantic flights with their DC-4s. Swissair's first four-engined airliner was HB-ILA *Genève*, a Douglas DC-4 delivered on 24 November 1946. In addition, four more DC-4s were delivered to Swissair as HB-ILE *Zürich*, HB-ILI *Basel*, HB-ILO *Luzern*, and HB-ILU *Unterwalden* (ex

Note the prominent fin de-icer boot on this Canadian Pacific DC-4   *M J Hooks*

C-54) and the type inaugurated Swissair's transatlantic service on 2 May 1947 under Captain Walter Borner. Surprisingly, although, perhaps, a sign of the times, some of Swissair's board members doubted the value of this twice-weekly operation and it was not until September 1949 that it was finally decided to make this trial service permanent. The DC-4 also opened up long-haul routes in other parts of the world, and became a mainstay of American domestic long-haul routes.

At the age of seven, I flew from Geneva to London in September 1948 in a Swissair DC-4. To fly in a large four-engined airliner in 1948 had a considerable *cachet*, when most other machines were twins. I had rheumatism at that time, and Swissair was supposed to provide a rug for the flight. The rug never materialised. But no matter. Because the DC-4 was heated and, in any case the flight was thrilling and I savour it even now half a century later.

The DC-4 was unpressurised, so we probably flew at around 8,000 ft, and, during the flight, I gazed down at recently war-torn France, slowly unfolding as we headed towards the channel at about 220 mph, to a background of muffled thunder from the engines cruising at about half power. A notice by a window intrigued me, "SORTIE DE SECOURS", i.e. "EMERGENCY EXIT" as I later discovered! During the weeks after the flight, when playing football, the noise of the wind in my ears as I hared round the pitch reminded me of the rising roar of the DC-4's Pratt & Whitney engines as they opened up for take-off.

Most of my contact with DC-4s was at Geneva airport, where Swissair and Air France DC-4s were regular visitors. Sometimes, the DC-4's engines would spit back through the carburettors at start up, showing a flash of yellow flame at the mouth of the air intake which was mounted on top of the engine nacelle. Luckily the intakes were forward facing, so nervous passengers were spared this worrying sight! As with other airliners of the day, a man with a portable fire extinguisher stood by, just in case, but I never saw an engine catch fire at start up.

But there was the odd incident. On one occasion, it was obvious that a Swissair DC-4 which had just taken off was having undercarriage problems, because the wheels stayed firmly down when they should have been retracting. Then, eventually, they retracted and the DC-4 went into a circuit with the obvious intention of landing, the wheels popped down

Swisssiar's DC-4 HB-ILA gets under way from Geneva   *M J Hooks*

again and the large machine landed with fire engines and rescue vehicles ranged beside the runway, presumably in case the undercarriage collapsed. But all was well and the DC-4 landed safely. However, as it taxied in, I noticed liquid dripping from a wing, and wondered if fuel had been jettisoned to get the aircraft down to a safe landing weight. This was about 1956. The photograph on the left shows Swissair's much-photographed DC-4 HB-ILA *Genève* just after take off with the wheels retracting forwards, as can clearly be seen. This was Swissair's first DC-4, delivered on 24 November 1946.

The DC-4 was noisy in the manner of most large piston-engined airliners, although relative to some of its contemporaries it was quite civilised,

Japan Air Lines operated DC-4s, which, as C-54s, were on the other side during WW2 *M J Hooks*

especially when compared to the Lockheed Constellation with jet-stack exhausts. The photographer taking the shot on the previous page of HB-ILA taking off will not be blocking his ears – not out of bravado; it wouldn't have been necessary.

Large airliners did not usually indulge in low flying during the 'fifties any more than they do now, both on safety and environmental grounds. But I had no complaints when, standing in a field near Dane Hill in Sussex, I heard the thrilling noise of a large low-flying aircraft approaching, unbelievably the familiar noise of a DC-4 of all things. And, sure enough, an Air France DC-4 hove into view and charged overhead. Even now, I can't imagine why this DC-4 should have been flying so low, so far from Heathrow.

The DC-4's Pratt & Whitney R-2000s were 14-cylinder aircooled two-row radials displacing 2000 cubic ins (hence its R-2000 designation) i.e. 32.8 litres, and this engine was essentially an enlarged version of the well-tried R-1830 radial whose best known home was in the DC-3. The R-2000 had the same 5.5 inch stroke as its R-1830 parent, but a larger bore of 5.75 ins compared to the smaller engine's 5.5 ins. Both engines were supercharged, as one would expect from a large piston engine, and both peaked at 2,700 rpm for take-off, for which the DC-4's R-2000 gave off 1,450 hp.

The DC-4 installation had an exhaust collector ring discharging through a substantial and very visible pipe outboard of each engine, which helped take the harshness out of the exhaust, and prevented a line of sight to the passengers to keep cabin noise down; the flaming discharge was very noticeable at night, but only to external observers as the exhaust was hidden from the occupants! Despite their strong similarities, the DC-4's R-2000 sounded quite different to the DC-3's R-

Canadair produced Merlin versions of the DC-4. BOAC called its machines Argonauts *MAP*

The Carvair car ferry looks too ungainly to fly *MAP*

1830, possibly because of their different propeller rpm – although I thought the exhaust beat sounded different too. So far as I know, the only other aircraft to use the R-2000 engine apart from the DC-4 was the twin-engined Canadian DHC Caribou bush transport.

The DC-4 carried 44 passengers, cruised at 227 mph at 10,000 ft and its range, varying with payload, made it long-legged enough for commercial transatlantic operations. However, an eight to 10 hour non-stop Atlantic crossing in a noisy piston-engined aircraft was a tiring experience, and it is said that Irish coffee was concocted to fortify passengers before they took off from Shannon for the long-haul across the pond. Who knows, it might have been the DC-4, or possibly the Constellation, which was the direct cause of Irish coffee!

An interesting variant of the DC-4 was the Canadair-built aircraft powered by Rolls-Royce Merlins. The Merlin was used because it could be imported to Canada, a British Commonwealth country, free of customs duty, while duty would have been paid on the Pratt & Whitney R-2000 from the USA. Also, the Merlin was chosen to give a performance increase over the Pratt & Whitney-powered DC-4. The 27 litre Merlin was smaller than the 32.8 litre R-2000, yet it was more powerful, giving 1,760 hp against 1,450 hp, increasing cruising speed from the DC-4's 227 mph to 289 mph. The DC-4M should have been called "the airliner that sounds like a bomber", because its Merlins gave it a military sound more in keeping with the Lancaster than a civil machine.

The unpressurised DC-4M prototype first flew in July 1946 with 1,725 hp Merlin 620s. There were three production versions, the unpressurised C-54GM North Star for the RCAF, which received 23 aircraft, the pressurised DC-4M-2 which went to TCA (20), and the pressurised Canadair C-4 for BOAC (22) and CPA (4). Among other routes, TCA's DC-4M-2s were used on transatlantic services. BOAC called its machines Argonauts, and 22 machines were delivered between March and November 1949 as G-ALHC to 'HP (*Ariadne, Ajax, Argo, Atlas, Aurora, Attica, Antares, Arcturus, Atalanta, Altair, Antaeus, Argosy, Amazon* and *Aethra*), and G-AHLR to 'HY (*Antiope, Astra, Athena, Artemis, Adonis, Aeolus, Astraea, Arian*), and they entered service on routes to the Far East, Middle East and South America.

A DC-4 used by NASA, possibly for research purposes *M J Hooks*

It was Argonaut G-ALHK *Atalanta* in which Princess Elizabeth left on 31 January 1952 on her Royal Tour of South Africa. *Atalanta* brought her back on 7 February as Queen Elizabeth II, when her father King George VI died while she was away.

When I first saw a DC-4M in 1947, flying quite low over Chobham, Surrey, on its way to Heathrow, presumably, I was intrigued at the warlike noise made by this peaceful looking machine. But one soon got used to the sound of Merlins in an airliner thanks to BOAC's

The prototype DC-6, built to replace the DC-4 for competing with the Connie   *B Robertson*

22 Argonauts which became a common sight and sound. However, use of the liquid-cooled Merlin in an airliner was swimming against the engineering tide, since aircooled radials were used exclusively in other large modern airliners (except in the unsuccessful Avro Tudor, which also had Merlins), and, at 27 litres, the Merlin was relatively small to power a large airliner. Initially there were problems with the Merlin's cooling system, which Rolls-Royce cured, but liquid cooling was a maintenance item, whereas air cooling was not. But that was not all. I remember listening to my crystal radio set one evening, prodding the cats whisker around to get good reception, and coming across a news bulletin saying that a BOAC Argonaut had returned to Heathrow that day because of "flames coming from the exhaust of an engine"! Perhaps this was caused by a burnt exhaust valve, and it must have been terrifying for the passengers. The roar from the inboard exhaust stubs was too much for passengers, although ex-Lancaster crews probably loved it, and a crossover exhaust system was installed directing all exhaust outboard of each engine nacelle. This meant some red-hot plumbing within the engine nacelle, but it seemed to work well and, from outside, made the Merlin sound smoother and higher pitched. BOAC stopped using Argonauts in 1960.

When a vehicle ferry was needed to replace the Bristol Super Freighter 32, there were plenty of used DC-4s around at good prices. So the Aviation Traders (Engineering) firm designed a car-ferry conversion for the DC-4 as being the only affordable way of meeting the need, because a new purpose-built aircraft would have been too expensive.

One of Sabena's DC-6s taxying out for take-off (note the flap angle)   *M J Hooks*

The DC-4 was modified for nose-loading of cars, and the hideous, if practical, result can be seen on page 10. Other mods were made, and the revised machine, known as the Carvair, first flew on 21 June 1961. The Carvair could carry five cars and 23 passengers, and it entered service with Channel Air Bridge on 1 March 1962. Twenty-one aircraft were converted and the type flew with various airlines over the years.

I was horrified at the laboured climb of a British United Carvair after take-off from Geneva in 1962. It looked most seriously underpowered, and very

The DC-6 production line at Santa Monica, California *M J Hooks*

cumbersome and I was glad not to be on it!

Towards the end of WW2, plans were prepared for the introduction of peacetime airline services in 1945, and although contemporary advertising could reasonably claim that "The Sun never sets on a Douglas Transport", the unpressurised DC-4, with its 1,450 hp engines and 230 mph cruise was no match for the pressurised Lockheed 049 Constellation, which had 2,200 hp engines, a 300 mph cruise and greater passenger capacity than the DC-4. Although a soundly engineered and reliable aircraft, the DC-4 was outdated by 1945 despite being quite new. The reason for the relatively high number of DC-4s being put into service when the war ended was probably because of the ready availability of cheap surplus C-54 military transports for

conversion to DC-4 airliners. However, long term, Douglas could only stay competitive by offering something better than the DC-4. Fortunately, the DC-4 was capable of being enlarged and developed into the pressurised DC-6, with 2,100 hp Pratt & Whitney R-2800 radials instead of the DC-4's 1,450 hp engines, and, although the DC-6 was introduced more than a year after the Connie, it turned out to be an effective competitor. Indeed, the DC-6's introduction started the colourful Lockheed-Douglas battle for commercial supremacy, which lasted until the late 'fifties before being prematurely snuffed out by the advent of jetliners.

The DC-6 prototype, shown at the top of page 11, first flew on 15 February 1946, and with its span of 117 ft 6 in and length of 100 ft 7 in, the new transport was about the same size as the competing Constellation which had corresponding dimensions of 123 ft and 95 ft 2 in respectively. While the DC-6 was not such a beautiful aircraft as the Connie, which had an attractive eel-shaped fuselage and graceful curved wingtips, the DC-6, with its parallel-sided fuselage and straight-tapered wings was pleasing in a functional sense.

The most obvious difference between the DC-6 and DC-4 was the new aircraft's fuselage, which was 6 ft 9 in longer, and because of this, the DC-6's passenger cabin windows continued aft of the passenger door which was located behind the wings. Other visible differences were minor and from some angles the two aircraft were virtually impossible to tell apart;

KLM's DC-6A in 'racing' trim during the England – New Zealand air race *B Robertson*

Swedish-registered DC-6 SE-BDG was delivered to SILA, a forerunner of SAS *M J Hooks*

the DC-6 even retained the general form of the Douglas nose and cockpit area first seen on the DC-1 in 1933. The installation of the DC-6's aircooled radials, like those of the DC-4, lacked the careful streamlining seen on some contemporary aircraft, being the minimum necessary to cowl each engine, cool it and fair it into the wing; only the most perfunctory attempt was made to blend the carburettor air intake and oil cooler into the nacelle. Two separate pairs of short pipes discharged the engine exhausts outboard of each nacelle which was scalloped to clear the gases, and although the outboard location helped to make the cabin noise bearable, the take-off noise was extremely harsh to onlookers. The DC-6 was much noisier than the DC-4, and, along with the Constellation with jet stack exhausts, was one of the noisiest piston airliners ever built.

DC-6 prototype alongside a military Super DC-3 *B Robertson*

DC-6s were first delivered on 24 November 1946 simultaneously to American Airlines and United Airlines, and services began after five months of route proving and training flights, thus starting a brilliant career for the aircraft. With a take-off weight of 97,200 lb, the new DC-6 weighted about 30 per cent more than its DC-4 parent. Accommodation varied between 48 and 86 passengers and the aircraft was one of the first airliners with a cruise in excess of the all-important 300 mph threshold.

An early problem with the DC-6 resulted in two in-flight fires in 1947. The aircraft used petrol-fired combustion heaters for cabin heating and de-icing; one heater in each outboard engine nacelle served the wings through leading edge ducting, a third

The Douglas-owned DC-6A N30006   *M J Hooks*

heater de-iced the tail unit, and cabin heat came from a unit under the passenger cabin floor.

Although petrol-fired heating in an aircraft sounds like a recipe for disaster, it turned out to be safe later on, and it was also used in other types of aircraft. However, initial problems with the DC-6 due to venting of fuel into the cabin heater air intake caused the fatal crash of United Airlines N37510. The aircraft came down at Bryce Canyon after nearly making a safe emergency landing; in a demonstration of *sang-froid*, the crew radioed reports right up until impact, and, tragically, their last words were "looks as though we might make it". Sadly, they didn't, and all passengers and crew were lost. But, an American Air Lines DC-6 was more fortunate, and Captain Chatfield managed to land, on fire, but safely, at Gallup, New Mexico, on 11 November 1947. All DC-6s were grounded for four months while the fault was cured, and the aircraft went back to work on 21 March 1948.

The DC-6 sold well both in the USA and overseas, and stayed in production for over four years; in addition to the prototype, 175 aircraft were built and all except one were sold to airlines in no less than ten countries, the single exception being supplied for presidential use in the USA as a C-118 and named *Independence*. Airlines in the USA bought 126 DC-6s and the largest orders came from United and American which took 50 and 46 aircraft respectively. Braniff received nine, one of which was the final DC-6 to be built and was delivered on 2 November 1951; seven went to Delta, and National and Panagra received eight and six respectively.

Delta, in common with other airlines, found that its DC-4s were completely outclassed by Constellations, which were much faster, and, unlike the DC-4, were pressurised and could therefore fly above the weather. Delta started DC-4 services on the important and newly-awarded 1,028 mile Chicago-Miami route on 6 March 1946, but little more than a year later, during the Summer of 1947, Eastern put its Connies on the same route. It was no contest for the DC-4. Delta's market share fell dramatically and the airline had no choice but to introduce Connies or DC-6s to stop a worrying loss of custom; in the event, DC-6s were chosen for a number of reasons, not least because Delta could not afford to be seen to follow Eastern's lead by operating Connies. Delta's seven DC-6s, N1901 to '7, offered pressurised travel to 56 passengers and the type entered service on 1 December 1948. But not before time, because the loss of passengers had become serious. Fortunately the DC-6s recovered Delta's market share and went on the serve the firm for the next 20 years.

Sabena bought five DC-6s, being the first foreign airline to take the type when OO-AWA was delivered in July 1947; in addition, eight were delivered to KLM, and 17 went to SAS. Linee Aeree Italiane (LAI), which merged with Alitalia in 1957, took four with the unlikely registrations I-LADY, I-LIKE, I-LOVE and I-LUCK – all's well that ends well, it seems! Outside Europe and the USA, six DC-6s went to Flota Aérea Mercante Argentina (FAMA), an airline which merged with three others to form Aerolineas Argentinas. Mexicana took three and Philippine Air Lines (PAL) bought five. The DC-6 proved to be an economical and reliable alternative to the Constellation, and its albeit less graceful parallel-sided fuselage

A US Navy R6D-1 gets off the ground. Note the added refinement of propeller spinners   *M J Hooks*

Douglas-owned DC-6A N30006 looks as though it is starting its take-off run   *B Robertson*

was much easier to stretch than the Connie's elegant curved fuselage. Douglas took advantage of the improved Pratt & Whitney R-2800-CB16 engine, uprated from the DC-6's R-2800-CA15 by 14 per cent to 2,400 hp, and stretched the DC-6 into the DC-6A, which made its maiden flight on 29 September 1949 as N30006. The DC-6A was a cargo aircraft with re-enforced flooring and two large cargo doors on the port side, one forward of the wing and the other aft. With the same wingspan as the DC-6, the DC-6A was longer by 5 ft, at 105 ft 7 in; its cargo capacity was 28,188 lb and its loaded weight rose from the DC-6's 97,200 lb to 107,000 lb.

Of the 75 DC-6As built, one was retained by Douglas, shown above and at the top of page 14, and 54 of them were sold in the USA. Slick Airways bought the first two N90807 and N908087, and went on to take ten more; the type went to American (ten), Flying Tiger (nine), Northeast (one), Pan American (three), Trans-Caribbean (four), United (seven) and one DC-6A was delivered to Riddle Airlines, an all-cargo airline. DC-6As also went to Los Angeles Air (two), Nevada Aero (two) and Overseas National (three); Canadian Pacific received five DC-6As and Maritime Central, also in Canada, took one aircraft. DC-6As were sold in Europe, where Airwork, Hunting-Clan, KLM and Sabena each took two. One of KLM's two machines, PH-TGA, is shown in "racing trim" at the bottom of page 12, taking part in the England to New-Zealand air race, complete with racing number 21 on its fin. Douglas surely never envisaged this when it designed the DC-6A! Further sales included one DC-6A which went to the Belgian Air Force, and another one to Swissair as HB-IBB on 2 October 1958; the final DC-6A delivery was made on 10 February 1959 to the Brazilian company Lóide Aéreo Nacional, which received four altogether.

The DC-6A shown below was one of two used machines which, in 1960, were fitted with special radar and instrumentation. They were flown by the US Department of Commerce Weather Bureau in a hurricane research program. Some DC-6As were converted for mixed cargo/passenger work as DC-6Cs.

This DC-6A was used by the US Dept of Commerce in a hurricane research programme   *B Robertson*

The highly-regarded DC-6B gave Lockheed some serious competition *B Robertson*

Discounting converted DC-6As, the final DC-6 development was the highly-regarded DC-6B passenger airliner which, with the same dimensions as the DC-6A was offered with either R-2800-CB16 engines of 2,400 hp each or with uprated

DC-6B interior, looking forward. Note the seating arrangement *M J Hooks*

2,500 hp R-2800-CB17s; interestingly, the CB17 was identical to the CB-16, but gave its extra power by running at a higher boost setting using 108/135 grade fuel, instead of the CB16's 100/130 grade; both engines had water injection to prevent detonation. The first DC-6B flew on 2 February 1951 as N37547, and this magnificent aircraft played its part in forcing Lockheed to stretch the Connie into the Super Constellation with its remarkable Wright Turbo Compound engines.

The DC-6B first went into service with American Airlines on 29 April 1951, and of the 287 DC-6Bs built, 283 were delivered to 29 airlines in an incredible 20 countries.

Douglas had, as usual, produced exactly what the airlines wanted, and the

DC-6B's impressive sales penetration was due to the aircraft's good combination of performance, reliability, operating economics and ease of maintenance.

The DC-6B gave an impression of brute power because of its austere appearance, its sheer size and its noisy engines. Thanks to its strong initial acceleration and the powerful bellow of its four Pratt & Whitneys, take-off in a DC-6B was a deeply satisfying, never to be forgotten experience.

To the occupants, the ground seemed to fall away quickly enough after take-off, but to onlookers on the ground the climb looked painfully slow,

Swissair's DC-6B HB-IBE *Genève* awaits passengers at Heathrow   *MAP*

in common with other contemporary large piston-engined airliners – in direct contrast to jetliners which simply leap off the deck, push their noses up to incredible angles and then ascend like lifts.

In the USA, the DC-6B was delivered to American (25), Continental (three), National (eight), Northeast (ten), Northwest (12), Panagra (four), Trans-American (seven), Western (31) and United, which took a massive 43 aircraft. However the largest number went to Pan American which received 45 between February 1952 and June 1954 and, in the traditional Pan American way, they were called Clippers. First to be delivered and put into service with Pan Am was N6519C, *Clipper Liberty Bell*, which joined the company on 27 February 1952 and inaugurated the all-tourist *Rainbow* service on the New York – London route on 1 May. The aircraft was fitted with 82 seats for this service, which was highly-packed compared to the 44-seat first class layout, and a transatlantic crossing – never the most restful of experiences in a large piston-machine - must have been a tiring ordeal in these DC-6Bs with their high-density seating. Pan Am's final DC-6B joined Pan Am as N50258K *Clipper Fair Wind* on 15 June 1954 and many of the airline's DC-6Bs were retained into the 'sixties, the last 15 being sold as late as September 1968.

Japan Air Lines bought two DC-6Bs, starting services with them on the Tokyo-San Francisco route in February 1954. Other airlines to take new DC-6Bs were Australian National Airways (four), Civil Air Transport of Taiwan (one), Ethiopian (three), LAN – Chile (seven) and Mexicana (two). The Canadian airline Maritime Central took one and Canadian Pacific received 13, starting operations with the type in 1955; two DC-6Bs went to PAL. Cathay Pacific's first brand new aircraft was a DC-6B (VR-HFK), which served with the company from 22 June 1958 to 29 November 1962, having joined a DC-6 and other types already in service with the airline.

Swissair became the first European airline to take delivery of DC-6Bs when HB-IBA *Zürich* joined the company on 24 June 1951, followed shortly afterwards by HB-IBE *Genève* on 18 July; both these aircraft served the airline for the next nine years after which they were sold to Sterling Airways of Copenhagen as OY-EAO and 'EAN, respectively, on 22 August and 16 June 1962. Four more DC-6Bs were delivered to Swissair, and the last one, HB-IBZ *Basel*, was sold on to Balair in December 1961.

Pan Am's DC-6B N6520C *Clipper Priscilla Alden* was one of 45 used by the airline   *B Robertson*

Sabena's DC-6B starts to taxi out to the runway for take-off   *MAP*

When British European Airways, with whom Swissair competed on its European routes, introduced its superb turboprop Viscounts in 1953, the aircraft caused considerable concern to Swissair which, at the time, was working its European routes with piston-engined Convair 240s – these aircraft had to give best to the Viscounts which were novel due their turbine engines; also, Viscounts were fast and relatively quiet, and offered excellent visibility for their passengers. However Swissair decided not to compete head on with BEA by buying Viscounts, and was able to meet the Viscount threat by putting its long-haul DC-6Bs on its European routes. And this may be why, just before Christmas in 1953, I found myself boarding a Swissair DC-6B at Heathrow bound for Geneva instead of the Convair 240, or even the ageing DC-3, that I was expecting.

I was aged 12, travelling on my own, and I shall never forget this flight. We were, as usual in those days, ferried out to the waiting aircraft in an airport coach and, to my horror, I found myself being decanted at the foot of the mobile stairway by one of Swissair's DC-6Bs. The aircraft towered above me, and as I climbed the stairway I wondered if I was boarding the wrong aircraft. Urgent enquiries to the air hostess elicited sweet reassurance that I wouldn't wake up in New York, and so, with considerable enthusiasm I settled into a window seat in this enormous and powerful aircraft. The engines started one by one, and such was the idling thrust of the four big Pratt & Whitneys, that the DC-6B jerked forward as the parking brakes were released; this incident heralded a brutishness about the aircraft which was to become evident in other ways. Also notable was the way in which the engines twisted back and forth about their propeller axes through a few degrees due to the uneven idling torque of the 18-cylinder engines. They must have been on flexible mountings to damp vibration, but it looked as though Douglas had a quality control problem!

I don't remember much about the pre-take off engine run up. But I shall never forget the take off, There was that feeling of pregnant expectancy as the DC-6B turned slowly to face down the runway, engines idling like the calm before the storm. With 10,000 hp I knew it was going to be impressive. And it was! The four engines opened out to take-off power with a harsh rising bellow, accompanied by a strong acceleration which pressed me back into my seat despite the fact that the aircraft was full. We thundered down the runway, and it must have looked and sounded magnificent to any

This Olympic Airways DC-6B taxis in after landing on its two inboard engines   *Olympic Airways*

A magnificent shot of SAS DC-6B OY-KMA   *M J Hooks*

onlookers, and I sat thrilled and tense in my seat as we accelerated up to flying speed, engines giving their full power. Then, the ground fell away, and I relaxed a little when the engines were eased back from take-off power to climb rating. I don't remember much of the rest of the flight. It was quite tame by comparison!

Another wild DC-6B experience, also with a Swissair machine, was a ground run to take-off power on one of the port engines close by the viewing area. It is probably the closest I have ever been to an aero engine running at take-off power, and one of the most exciting experiences of my life. It had been evident from the mechanics working on the engine that it had been giving trouble, and it was being ground run after being put right.

Another magnificent shot of an SAS DC-6B   *M J Hooks*

I was standing in front of the engine, probably about 25 yards away. There was no feeling of being sucked towards its propeller, although the fence separating the viewing area from the apron (yes, this took place on the apron!) may have been the reason. Also, with the exhaust facing backwards the sound, although furious and powerful, was bearable.

DC-6Bs were also delivered to KLM (seven), Olympic (three), Sabena (nine) and SAS (14); Transports Aériens Intercontinentaux (TAI) took five and Union Aéromaritime de Transport (UAT) received three. Six and four, respectively, were delivered to the two Italian

Pan Am's DC-6B N5028K Clipper Fairwind taxis in after landing on, as usual, two engines *MAP*

airlines, Alitalia and LAI; the final DC-6B was delivered on 17 November 1958 to Jugoslovenski Aerotransport, which received two as YU-AFA and YU-AFB.

No doubt there are many ex-DC-6B passengers who have their own memories of this outstanding aircraft. Those who took seven hours to travel from Switzerland to Heathrow in December 1951 will be among them as, thanks to fog over most of Europe, what should have been a straightforward two-hour hop from Geneva had to be made from the Swiss military airfield of Sion; this meant climbing out through a mountain valley in this large aircraft, an experience which was spectacular in more ways than one both for occupants and onlookers. After flying non-stop for six hours, during which several changes of destination were made owing to continually varying weather conditions, a landing was made at Manston and when the DC-6B finally touched down at Heathrow the passengers cheered the long suffering Swissair crew who had brought them safely home! One can only hope that the Swiss crew managed to get home in time for Christmas with their own families. During the flight, my mother asked if the DC-6B had enough petrol to stay up for so long, and an air hostess replied "Don't worry, we fly to New York in these aircraft"!

The DC-6 series became very well-known in numerous parts of the world, not least in the UK, especially to enthusiasts living within a reasonable distance from Heathrow. One summer morning, in Chobham, Surrey, I went out into the garden and, to my astonishment, heard the distant, but familiar noise of a DC-6 doing its pre-take off engine run up. Once heard never forgotten, and I knew exactly what this was. But the surprise was that I could hear it at all, because never had I heard an aircraft running up at Heathrow or Blackbushe before or since. These two airports were too far away, and there was too much in the way, in the form of trees, buildings and topography. So this DC-6 must have been a freak occurrence. The knowledgeable probably won't ask how I knew it was a DC-6 rather than a Convair – but I'll tell them anyway. Quite simply because the run up was that of a four-engined aircraft rather than a twin. The aircraft could have been a Breguet Provence, which also had Pratt & Whitney R-2800s, but DC-6s were far more numerous. Fairoaks airfield was a few miles down the road, but was for light aircraft and there was no way 'my' DC-6 could have been there.

After many years of absence, I heard, once again, the well remembered sound of four Pratt & Whitney R-2800 engines on 22 March 1988 over Bordon in Hampshire at 4.30 pm, and had the pleasure of seeing what was certainly G-SIXC or G-APSA. I have heard this sound many times since then, always with pleasure, and whenever possible I always rush out to look at its perpetrator – this large, harsh-sounding aircraft which, once, was such an everyday sight and one of the colourful contributors to the piston-engined commercial era.

Watching a DC-6 land was less dramatic than take off, but an interesting experience nevertheless. Most of my airport observations of DC-6s were at Geneva Cointrin. A typical occasion started with an announcement over the public address heralding an incoming DC-6B "Le DC-6B de la compagnie Swissair, venant to New York, atterit", and there was the distant, familiar, front view of a DC-6B approaching the runway on long finals, flaps and gear down. As the large descending machine got nearer, its engines could be heard, faintly at first but getting louder as the machine approached, running in fine pitch and sounding healthy and strong, right up until just before touch down when the note suddenly subsided to almost complete silence; there was a distant screech as the tyres kissed the concrete and the aircraft ran along the runway. Then, a harsh noise as the engines wound up again with propellers in reverse pitch to slow the aircraft down, followed by a snarling grumble from the idling engines now clearly audible across the open expanse of the airport as the DC-6B, brakes squealing noisily, turned slowly off the runway to taxi towards us at the airport buildings – usually with two of its four engines shut down.

Watching a DC-6 starting up was also an interesting experience. As with jetliners, each engine would be started one by one, but the difference between then and now was the man with the portable fire extinguisher at the ready, going from one engine to the next as it started up, in case of a flash back through the carburettor starting an induction fire. Fires did sometimes happen, but I never saw an instance – just an occasional flash of flame at the carburettor air intake. I know of a DC-4 which was destroyed by fire at start up. The propeller of the starting engine would revolve slowly and silently driven

Note the open cockpit windows on this Etheopian Air Lines colourful DC-6B *M J Hooks*

by the electric starter motor, and then would jerk and speed up as the engine fired, accompanied by blue exhaust smoke and an angry exhaust snarl, and a faint undulating whistle from the prop. All would fall silent again as the engine died, then it would catch and settle down to a snarling idle. The cycle was repeated for the other three engines, and the big previously-silent bird was now alive, ready to move off the apron to the run-up area by the mouth of the runway.

It was said in those days that the flight-deck tension before take-off could be cut with a knife. Perhaps it still can be. But the big difference between airliners then and now was the margin of power available to cover engine failure. Modern jetliners, with their rapid rate of climb, are clearly much better in this respect than the old piston airliners, for which an engine failure at take-off, even in a four–engined machine, could spell disaster. The problem was compounded by the fact that piston engines, although reliable, were less so than modern turbofan engines.

A welcome feature of the US market for home-grown manufacturers was the sizeable military requirement for transport aircraft, which provided a good demand for military versions of airliners. This market was tapped by Convair, Lockheed, Boeing and Douglas, which must have helped reduce unit costs thanks to the economies of scale. No DC-6s were built for the US military except the one-off presidential C-118-DO *Independence*. However, the USAF bought 101 military versions of the DC-6A (C-118A) as personnel and logistics transports for the USAF Military Air Transport Service (MATS). These aircraft had 2,500 hp Pratt & Whitney R-2800-52W engines and could, alternatively, carry 74 passengers, 60 stretcher cases or 27,000 lb of cargo. The US Navy, also, bought 65 versions of the DC-6A known as the R6D-1s for use by the US Navy Fleet Logistic Air Wings. Production of the military DC-6As was completed on 29 December 1955, making a total of 166 military versions.

In summary, the DC-6 was produced as competition to the Lockheed Constellation which, for over a year, was unique in its size class until the introduction of the DC-6. In the face of competition from the DC-6, Lockheed upgraded the Connie, and the original Model 049 gave way to the 649 which first flew in October 1946, about eight months after the DC-6's first flight, and then came the 749 Connie in 1947, followed by the 749A in 1949 – each new variant offering improvements over its predecessor. Douglas eventually replied in February 1951 with the DC-6B, an improved DC-6, a superb aircraft with the best operating economics of its class at the time of its introduction, and faster than the Connie. Lockheed's answer to the formidable DC-6B was to stretch the Connie into the Model 1049 Super Constellation, the prototype first flying in 1950 initially with stop-gap 2,800 hp Wright R-3350 engines as the intended 3,250 hp Wright Turbo Compounds were not ready at the time. The first civil Super Connie with Turbo Compound engines was the Model 1049C, which first flew on 17 February 1953.

A total of 704 examples of the DC-6 series were built. This compares with 233 of the competing Constellation in all its forms - a good production run, but the fact remains that DC-6 series production was over three times as high as that of the Connie, and, furthermore, while the Connie went out of production in 1951, the DC-6B stayed in production until 1958. The DC-6B was probably the best all-round piston-engined airliner ever built – and it was probably the noisiest! In the meantime, responding to an American Airlines requirement, Douglas developed the DC-6B into the DC-7, powered, like the 1049C Super Connie, by the remarkable Wright Turbo Compound radial.

The severe, business-like shape of SAS DC-6B OY-KMA is well-shown in this photo   *M J Hooks*

This engine was notable for its power recovery turbines driven by exhaust gases and geared to the crankshaft through fluid couplings, increasing power by 20 per cent from 2,700 hp to 3,250 hp. There were three turbines, each of which was fed with exhaust from six of the engine's 18 cylinders, and, as a result of the energy extracted by the turbines, the exhaust became astonishingly quiet – in sharp contrast to the harsh roar from the DC-6B's Pratt & Whitney R-2800s. Also, the DC-7's 13 ft 6 in diameter four-blade propellers were quiet due to a relatively modest tip speed of M 0.803 at sea-level, whereas the Super Connie's larger diameter (15 ft 2 in) three-bladers were very noisy with their higher tip-speed of M 0.902. Indeed, the DC-7's combination of quiet exhaust and quiet propellers put it almost in the turboprop category for silent running. My impression was that the DC-7 made less noise at take-off than the turboprop Viscount, even if it was inferior to the Britannia in quiet running. The Viscount/DC-7 comparison may surprise readers, but I believe it to be true.

The DC-6B was a very large airliner in its day (N6519C)   *B Robertson*

The DC-7 was Douglas' answer to the Super Connie, somewhat belated as the prototype Super Connie first flew in 1950, whereas the decision to develop the DC-7 was not taken until January 1952. American Airlines ordered 25 DC-7s worth a total of $40 million. Douglas was unconvinced that the DC-7 would sell, but the American Airlines order got the DC-7 off the ground, and the airline paid for most of the development costs.

The DC-7 was, essentially, a stretched DC-6B with the new Wright Turbo Compound engine, and, as such, looked very similar to its DC-6B parent. It shared its 117 ft 6 in span with the DC-6B (and, indeed with the DC-6 and DC-4), but the DC-7's

Even Cunard Eagles colourful livery cannot hide the DC-6B's severe lines   *M J Hooks*

length was 108 ft 11 in compared to the DC-6B's length of 105 ft 7 in. An obvious difference between the DC-7 and the DC-6B was the former's four-blade propellers, whereas the DC-6B had three-bladers. Despite being barely larger than the DC-6B, the DC-7's take-off weight, at 122,200 lb, was 15 per cent more than for the DC-6B. Also, the DC-7's Wright Turbo Compounds gave the DC-7 a massive 30 per cent more power, and when it first flew it was little wonder that the *Colliers* magazine (or it may have been the *Saturday Evening Post*) said that "No other US airliner flies so fast". And fast it was, being the first production piston-engined airliner to reach 400 mph, a most impressive speed for a large piston-engined aircraft in 1952.

Douglas persisted in retaining a single nosewheel on the DC-7 long after other major manufacturers went over to twin nosewheels, a quaint connection with the original DC-4E of 1938. The DC-7C's passenger capacity rose from the DC-6B's 54 to 60 in standard form. It is worth bearing in mind that the DC-7 had the same wing area as its DC-4 grandparent, yet it weighed 67 per cent more, had well over twice the power and was 46 per cent faster! This was the ultimate development of the basic DC-4 concept, and a most impressive one it was too. Douglas supporters will have noticed that the DC-7's top speed exceeded that of Lockheed's competing Super Constellation! I had got to recognise the noise of the Wright Turbo Compounds from seeing Fairchild C-119 Packet twin-boom transports, some versions of which were powered by TCs, and, when I saw my 'first' DC-7, I recognised the Turbo Compound engine noise at once.

Douglas reluctantly developed the DC-7 at the request of American Airlines   *M J Hooks*

An obvious difference between DC-6B and the DC-7 was the latter's four-blade propellers   *M J Hooks*

Douglas went to some lengths to spare passengers from the DC-6B's harsh exhaust note, by arranging exhaust discharge outboard of the engine nacelles. But this was considered unnecessary on the DC-7 thanks to the Turbo Compound's quiet exhaust note, and so exhausts discharged both inboard and outboard of the engines. In the photograph at the top of the next page, the outboard exhausts, just behind the open cooling air gills, can be seen as two short pipes; there was a similar arrangement inboard. This made for easier exhaust plumbing within the engine cowling, but it meant that the night exhaust flames could be seen by the passengers, not a few of whom were terrified of what they saw, believing the engines to be on fire. Oh, the joys of air travel during the piston days – and nobody bothered to tell you!

Indeed, one passenger whom I know was so frightened doing a night take-off in a DC-7C, and, not wanting to make a fool of herself, said through clenched her teeth to the passenger next to her that things "didn't seem quite right with the engines!". He managed to reassure her that nocturnal fireworks were "quite normal". Nowadays, with the accent on safety customer care and lawsuits for everything under the sun, airlines would probably issue pre-flight reassurances about exhaust flames during night flights. No flames are visible nowadays, except on Concorde.

The prototype DC-7 towers above the two ground staff   *M J Hooks*

The two men standing under the starboard outer engine of the DC-7 in the picture on the left give an impression of the aircraft's size, and the sheer bulk of the engines is notable, as are the four-bladed propellers with their dark-coloured leading edge de-icer pads. However, compared to a Boeing 747, the DC-7 is quite small.

The DC-7 first flew on 18 May 1953, and American Airlines

The mighty DC-7C was able to cross the Atlantic both ways non-stop *B Robertson*

introduced the type on the New York to Los Angeles service on 29 November 1953. The DC-7 was not sold outside the USA, and was bought by American Airlines which took 34 machines, Delta (10), National (4), and United took a massive 57 aircraft! Delta introduced its 69 passenger *Golden Crown* DC-7s to compete with Eastern's Super Connies, and N4871C *Royal Biscayne* was delivered on 22 February 1954, with the remaining machines coming over the next 13 months as N4872C to '80C. Delta inaugurated DC-7 services on 1 April 1954. National, too, used DC-7s to compete with Eastern's Super Connies; National put its DC-7Cs to work on 15 December 1953. To the British, who were developing the turboprop Britannia, the DC-7, while impressive, was nevertheless a piston machine in a turbine age.

Unfortunately, the price sometimes paid for engineering complexity is reliability, and thus it was with the DC-7's complex Turbo Compound engines with their power recovery turbines, which gave airline engineering staff some problems. I think it is true to say that the Turbo Compounds never achieved the reliability of the DC-6B's much simpler, if lower powered, Pratt & Whitney R-2800s. Looking at the night flames from the exhaust, it was a sobering thought that the power recovery turbines were operating in a searing sea of flame, running at 19,000 rpm at take-off; so, not surprisingly, the turbines had to be aircooled to keep metal temperatures within acceptable limits. Also, there was the additional complexity of connecting the turbines to the crankshaft though reduction gearing and shock-absorbing hydraulic couplings – one has to sympathise with DC-7 maintenance staff who were called upon to make sure that aircraft were on the ramp and ready to go when required. Nevertheless, the Turbo Compound was used in several aircraft, and was commercially successful but, unfortunately, Wright Aeronautical failed to develop a replacement engine at a time when piston engines were growing obsolete. During that time Wright should have been developing turbine engines for the forthcoming generation of jetliners, and, in this, it completely missed the boat, leaving the market to Pratt & Whitney, General Electric and Rolls-Royce.

Competition between Douglas and Lockheed forced the pace of development of both Super Connie and DC-7. KLM started transatlantic services with its Super Connie 1049Cs, the first civil Super Connie variant with Wright Turbo Compounds, in August 1953. These days, we take non-stop transatlantic services between major European centres and New York in both directions for granted. But this was not always the case. Introduction of its 1049C enabled KLM to fly non-stop eastbound from New York to Amsterdam, while, for the westbound trip, prevailing winds made a stop at Shannon or Prestwick necessary for fuel. This was a major step forward in transatlantic flying, but the ultimate goal was non-stop flights in both directions. It was to be two years before KLM's performance could be matched by the DC-7, in the form of the DC-7B. This DC-7 development could be had with increased fuel capacity in rearwards extended engine nacelles, and increased take-off weight from the DC-7's 122,200 lb to 126,000 lb, although there was no power increase. Pan Am and SAA opted for the extra tankage in its DC-7Bs and Pan Am started transatlantic services on 13 June 1955, non-stop New York - London, two years after KLM's Super Connie 1049Cs. But, like the 1049Cs, Pan Am's DC-7Bs could not fly the Atlantic non-stop in the westbound direction.

The DC-7B first flew in October 1954 (N70D), and the type went to Panagra, Eastern, Delta, Pan Am, American, Continental, National and SAA. TWA introduced the 1049G version of the Super Constellation on the Atlantic run two months after Pan Am's DC-7Bs, on 1 November 1955. Rather brashly known as the Super G, the 1049G had greater range than its predecessors, and could cross the Atlantic non-stop in both directions under favourable weather conditions. So Pan Am and TWA competed with one another on the North Atlantic run with DC-7Bs and 1049Gs respectively. But competitive pressure was on for non-stop transatlantic services in both directions regardless of prevailing wind conditions,

Swissair's DC-7Cs had a short innings and were replaced by DC-8 jetliners   *Swissair*

and, at Pan Am's request in 1954 for a development of the DC-7, Douglas developed the DC-7C, the mighty Seven Seas, which was the first airliner able to do the transatlantic run non-stop in either direction against prevailing winds.

Douglas now had the advantage over Lockheed's Model 1049G Super Connie, when Pan Am put the DC-7C to work on 1 June 1956. Extra fuel was carried in a wing of increased span. A centre section without dihedral was added up to the inboard engines, and to counter criticism of noise in its predecessors, the engines were moved outboard. There was also a power increase from the DC-7 and DC-7B's 3,250 hp per engine to a massive 3,400 hp from the uprated Wright Turbo Compound 18EA1 driving quiet-running Hamilton Standard four-blade propellers.

An obvious competitor for the DC-7C was the turboprop Bristol Britannia, and, indeed, it is quite likely that had the Britannia not been delayed by engine problems, then it might have taken a sizeable share of the market which went, by default, to Lockheed and Douglas. BOAC, a major Britannia operator, caused surprise and dismay in 1955 when it ordered

BOAC bought ten DC-7Cs as an insurance against problems with the Bristol Britannia   *B Robertson*

KLM was one of several European airlines operating DC-7Cs   *M J Hooks*

10 DC-7Cs as an insurance against late delivery of its Britannia fleet. As it turned out, this was a wise decision, because the following year the Britannia hit unexpected engine problems which took about 10 months to cure – this was a long time in the airliner market of the day and prevented the Britannia from becoming a really major seller.

The picture opposite shows BOAC's first DC-7C, G-AOIA, delivered in October 1956. BOAC's 10 DC-7Bs were delivered between October 1956 and April 1957 as G-AOIA to 'IJ. But this was the tail end of the propliner era, with

This DC-7C's centre section will eventually be offered up to the fuselage   *M J Hooks*

This looks like an open day at the Douglas plant, as people walk by DC-7Cs under construction *M J Hooks*

jetliners just round the corner in the form of the Boeing 707, Douglas DC-8 and Comet 4, and BOAC's DC-7Cs, like those of other airlines, had a relatively short innings as first line long-haulers, and were disposed of between 1963 and 1965.

I was plane watching with some friends at Heathrow one fine day in 1961, and I said that the livery of BOAC's DC-7Cs, and its other aircraft, seemed rather dull compared to the more colourful aircraft of other airlines – however, my fellow watchers found BOAC's livery to be pleasantly restrained and much to their liking compared to some of the more colourful foreigners, such as KLM's machine shown above, one of 15 bought by the Dutch airline.

A KLM DC-7C might look small today – it was enormous during the 'fifties *M J Hooks*

DC-7Cs were bought by Pan American (25), SAS (14), Swissair (5), Braniff (7), BOAC (10), Panair do Brasil (3), Mexicana (4), Sabena (10), KLM (15), Northwest (4), Alitalia (6), TAI (3) and JAL (4). Swissair's aircraft were HB-IBK, to 'IBN, and HB-IBP (*Zürich, Genève, Basel-Stadt, Bern, Schwyz*). *Schwyz*

The DC-7C and Starliner brought the colourful piston era to an end, to be replaced by jetliners *M J Hooks*

had a remarkably short innings with Swissair of only three years, being delivered on 4 November 1958 and being sold to SAS as SE-CCH on 5 November 1961. Pan Am's 25 DC-7Cs, in the airline's tradition, were christened with names prefixed by *Clipper* (e.g. *Clippers Black Hawk, Ganges, Midnight Sun, Rainbow*, etc). *Clipper Swansong*, if used, would have been an apt name, because the DC-7C marked the magnificent swansong of the piston era, sharing it with the Lockheed Model 1649 Starliner – built to compete with the DC-7C.

Unfortunately for Lockheed, the Starliner entered service a year later than the DC-7C, on 1 June 1957, so the DC-7 scooped most of the market during the twilight days of the piston era, and, because the Starliner was so close to the end of the piston era with the imminent arrival of jetliners, the market was foreclosing on propliners and the Starliner was only bought by Air France and Lufthansa. And so came to an end one of the most colourful periods of commercial aviation, a time when the piston engined airliner had reached a high degree of development, able to fly non-stop safely and reliably between European capitals and the new world as a matter of routine.

About seven years into the jetliner era, in 1965, when the DC-7 and its variants had long been made obsolete as first-line long-haulers, there was a fascinating, if horrifying experiment in which a redundant DC-7 was used to investigate (I believe) methods of increasing passenger survivability in the event of a crash – with dummies, naturally!. The unmanned DC-7 was deliberately crashed during take off, before leaving the ground, and the sequence was shown on television both from outside and inside the aircraft.

But to end on a more positive note, let's have a look at how it sometimes was. An airliner just in from New York taxis up to the buildings of a major European airport. Idling engines are cut, and immediately a team of ground staff converge on the now silent bird to prepare it for its next flight. A mobile stairway is manoeuvred up to the airliner and a celebrity appears framed in the open doorway, stepping forward to pose for the waiting photographers. The VIP then slowly descends the stairway, perhaps to run the gauntlet of the press, or to be whisked off in a limousine. This was part of the glamour of the 'fifties, when to have just 'flown in' from the States had a certain *cachet* which is absent from modern flying. And part of this *cachet* were the magnificent Douglas and Lockheed aircraft which made such flights possible – the *corps d'élite* of their time.

* * * * * * * * * * * * *

Technical Data

DOUGLAS DC-4-1009[1]

Manufacturer: The Douglas Aircraft Company, Santa Monica, California, USA.

Type: Four-engined long and medium-haul airliner.

Wings: Cantilever low-wing monoplane. Straight-tapered wing with stressed-skin all-metal structure.

Tail unit: Cantilever monoplane type with single fin. All-metal structure, except fabric-covered elevators and rudder.

Fuselage: All-metal structure.

Accommodation: Flight crew of four and cabin attendants. Normal capacity 44 passengers; high density configuration up to 86 passengers later on. Unpressurised accommodation.

Engines: Four Pratt & Whitney R-2000 fourteen cylinder aircooled radial engines. Hamilton Standard Hydromatic constant-speed propellers through 0.5:1 reduction gear. Each propeller has three blades and feathering capability, but no reversible pitch. Each engine gives 1,450 hp for take-off.

Landing Gear: Retractable tricycle landing gear has one wheel on nose leg (steerable) and twin-wheels on each main leg. Hydraulic retraction, hinging forwards, mainwheels into inboard engine nacelles.

Dimensions: Span 117 ft 6 in (35.81 m), length 93 ft 10 in (28.60 m), height 27 ft 6 in (8.38 m). Wing area 1,460 ft^2 (135.64 m^2).

Weights & Loadings: Empty 43,300 lb (19,640 kg). Maximum weight 73,000 lb (33,113 kg).

Performance: Maximum speed 280 mph (451 km/h) @ 14,000 ft (4,267 m); cruise 227 mph (365 km/h) @ 10,000 ft (3,048 m). Range 2,500 miles (4,023 km) with a payload of 11,400 lb (5,170 kg).

1. This was the designation of the 79 new DC-4s built post-WW2.

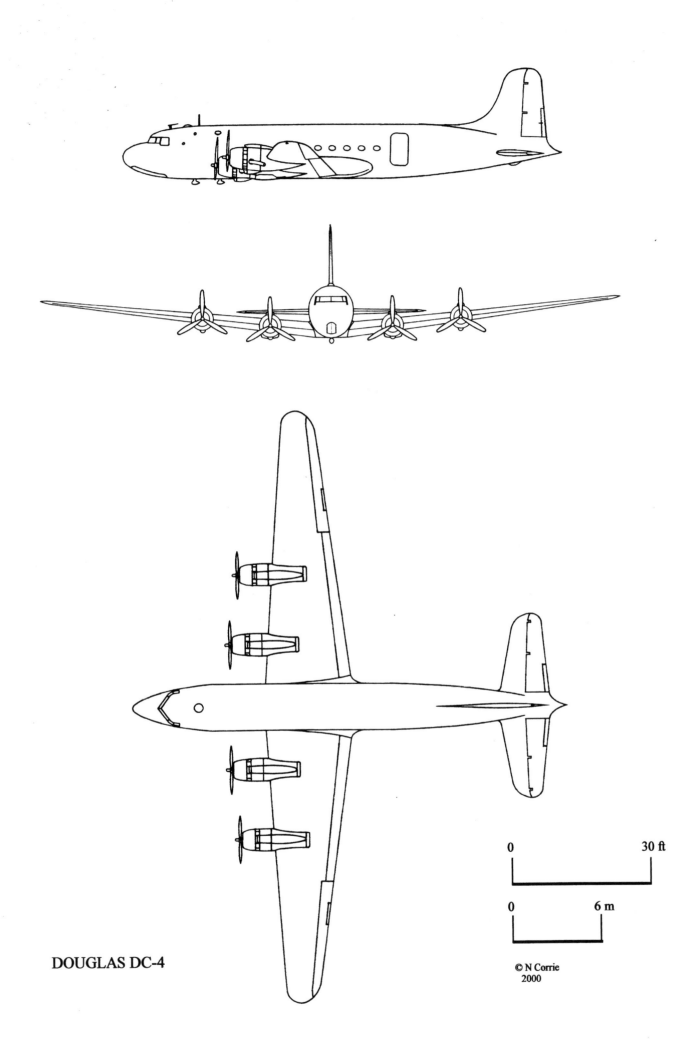

DOUGLAS DC-4

0   30 ft

0   6 m

© N Corrie
2000

Technical Data

Pratt & Whitney R-2000 2SD13-G Engine

Manufacturer:
Pratt & Whitney Aircraft, Hartford, Connecticut, USA.

Type:
14-cylinder aircooled two-row radial engine with spark ignition.

Cylinders:
Bore 146 mm, stroke 139.5 mm (32.7 litres). Cast aluminium head screwed and shrunk on to each forged steel cylinder barrel. Forged aluminium sleeve with integral cooling fins is shrunk on to each cylinder barrel. Inserts for valve seats are shrunk into head. Compression ratio 6.5:1.

Pistons:
Forged aluminium pistons, each with three compression rings, pair of dual oil control rings and one oil scraper ring.

Connecting Rods:
Each cylinder row has master rod; six auxillary rods are connected to each master rod by knuckle pins.

Crankshaft:
Two-throw one-piece crankshaft is supported by three plain lead-silver bearings.

Crankcase:
Main crankcase (power section) comprises three forged and machined aluminium sections bolted together.

Valvegear:
Two pushrod-operated valves per cylinder, with sodium-cooled stellite-faced exhaust valves. Pushrods actuated by two cam rings, one per cylinder row, driven at one eighth crankshaft speed through spur gears from the crankshaft.

Induction:
Two-speed single-stage supercharger is fitted at rear of engine. Centrifugal impeller is driven by spring-loaded flexible shock-absorbing drive. Gear changing is carried out by cone clutches. Step-up ratio for low gear is 7.15:1, and for high gear is 9.52:1. Petrol-air mixture is supplied by Stromberg carburettor with automatic mixture control and priming facility.

Lubrication:
Dry-sump system with forced feed throughout engine by gear-type pump.

Ignition:
Spark ignition system fitted, comprising two independent magneto-energised systems.   Two Scintilla magnetos are mounted at front of engine. Two spark plugs per cylinder.

Propeller Drive:
Reduction gear of 0.5:1 ratio.

Dimensions:
Diameter 49.1 in (1.25 m).

Dry Weight:
1,605 lb (728 kg).

Performance:
Take-off power: 1,450 hp @ 2,700 RPM. Normal rated power (i.e. maximum climb power): 1,200 hp (low blower) @ 5,000 ft (1,524 m), 1,100 hp (high blower) @ 14,000 ft (4,267 m), both outputs @ 2,550 RPM.